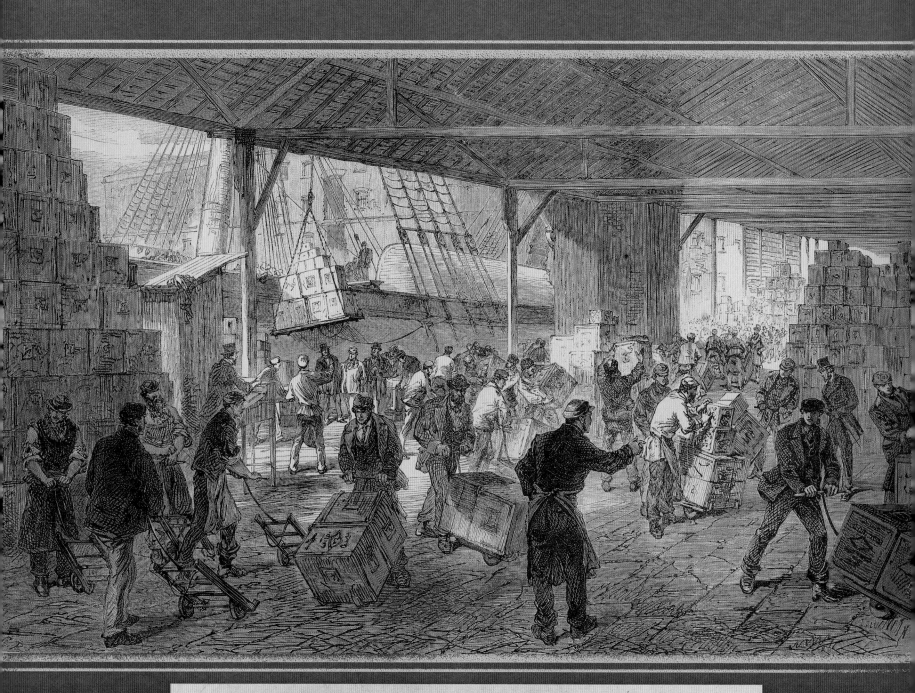

Unloading Tea-Ships on the East India Docks, London, England (1867), wood engraving.

America's Tea Parties

NOT ONE BUT FOUR!

BOSTON ✳ CHARLESTON ✳ NEW YORK ✳ PHILADELPHIA

ABRAMS BOOKS FOR YOUNG READERS · NEW YORK

BY MARISSA MOSS

Library of Congress Cataloging-in-Publication Data

Moss, Marissa.
America's tea parties : not one but four! : Boston, Charleston, New York, Philadelphia / by Marissa Moss.
pages cm
ISBN 978-1-4197-1874-8
1. Boston Tea Party, Boston, Mass., 1773—Juvenile literature.
2. United States—History—Revolution, 1775–1783—Causes—Juvenile literature.
3. Tea tax (American colonies)—Juvenile literature. I. Title.
E215.7.M68 2016
973.3'115—dc23
2015014051

Text copyright © 2016 Marissa Moss
Book design by Jessie Gang
For illustration credits, see page 47.

Printed and bound in China
10 9 8 7 6 5 4 3 2 1

Abrams Books for Young Readers are available at special discounts when purchased in quantity for premiums
and promotions as well as fundraising or educational use. Special editions can also be created to specification.
For details, contact specialsales@abramsbooks.com or the address below.

THE ART OF BOOKS SINCE 1949

115 West 18th Street
New York, NY 10011
www.abramsbooks.com

To Adam and to Julius Lester,
in gratitude for his help

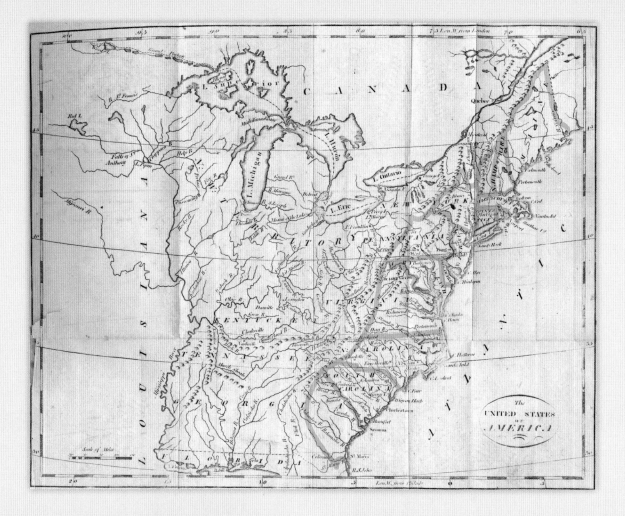

A map of the original thirteen colonies and territories (detail at right). The colonies are Connecticut, Delaware, Georgia, Maryland, Massachusetts (which included what later became the state of Maine), New Hampshire, New Jersey, New York, North Carolina, Pennsylvania, Rhode Island, South Carolina, and Virginia and are hand-drawn by the author over an original 1799 map.

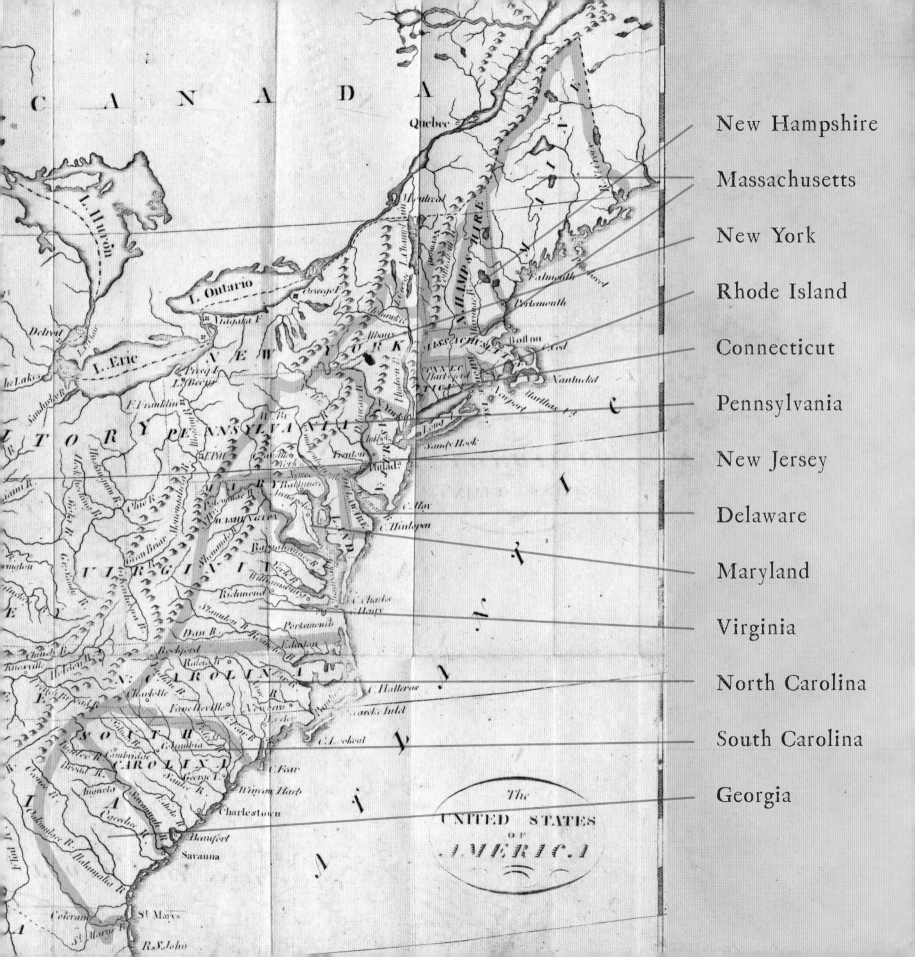

New Hampshire

Massachusetts

New York

Rhode Island

Connecticut

Pennsylvania

New Jersey

Delaware

Maryland

Virginia

North Carolina

South Carolina

Georgia

Destruction of Tea at Boston Harbor, a lithograph published in 1846 by Sarony & Major, showing colonists dressed as Indians.

**I**t all started with seven ships and 2,202 chests of tea. (Divide 2,202 by 7, and you'll discover the average number of chests per ship.) That's almost 550,000 pounds of tea, worth around 5 million dollars. (For extra credit, divide 5 million by 7 and you'll see what the average cargo was worth per ship.) Take all those numbers and divide them by the pride and determination of the thirteen American colonies, and you get a mountain of tea dumped into the ocean.

Not all the tea was destroyed. A small amount was smuggled into merchants' homes, and most was sent back to England, untouched and untaxed. That still left 426 chests of tea steeping in colonial harbors for the fish to drink. This is the story of all those chests and the welcome they received from four tea parties. That's right—not just the one in Boston that everyone still talks about but *four*!

Before the tea parties, though, came the tax, and before the tax came the East India Company. Despite the name, this was an English corporation, one that was closely tied to the government. Established as a major importer of spices and goods from India, the East India Company had been granted special license by the British Crown to mint money, acquire territory, maintain a standing army, enter into wars, and negotiate peace. The Company ruled India like a private estate—a government within the British government. Imagine a *company* today being allowed to make money and control territory with its own military!

Above: Sealing wax and a stamp, like those used to seal official papers and authenticate documents. Below: Symbol of the East India Company.

With all that freedom and power, the East India Company should have been wealthy. And indeed it had been. But with great wealth comes great temptation. And great temptation often leads to gross corruption. That's what happened to the Company. Like robbers entrusted with guarding a bank, its greedy directors filled their own pockets, thereby starving the corporation of cash. Since the Bank of England (a privately owned bank that handled most of the government's finances) was always ready to lend the Company more money, that wasn't a problem. Whenever the Company ran low on cash, the bank happily provided large loans . . . which put the Company even deeper into debt.

And then things got worse with the bank recession of 1772, when a credit scare caused a run on banks. People withdrew their money because they were afraid the banks would collapse . . . and all these withdrawals caused the very collapse the public feared. (It was like what happened nearly two centuries later during the Great Depression in the United States: So many people rushed to get their savings that many banks were emptied out, ruined.) The Bank of England survived, propped up by the government, but it was teetering so much that it couldn't risk giving any more large loans to the East India Company.

By then, the Company owed the Bank of

The India-man wrecked. L. 12.

Treasury Cape

Shah Allum in Distress. This political cartoon from 1773 shows the East India Company on the verge of bankruptcy. "Shah Allum" refers to Sir George Colebrook, a director who was faulted for steering the company into a financial shipwreck.

England 300,000 pounds sterling (the equivalent of approximately 30 million dollars today) and owed the British government more than a million pounds in taxes and annual payments. The

A coffee house in colonial America. Coffee drinking was viewed as a rejection of the English tax on tea.

Company should have declared bankruptcy. It should have failed. But King George III couldn't let that happen. Not only would it have been horribly embarrassing, but who would then run the colony of India? So Parliament came up with a plan—something the American colonists called "a ministerial plot," which sounds much more evil.

The only way for the East India Company to get out of its huge mountain of debt was to sell more of its principal product: tea. And the biggest market it could expand into was the American colonies, where tea was the most popular hot drink and the fourth-largest British import (the first three were cloth, sugar, and salt). But it could be even bigger. Although the colonists drank 1.2 million pounds of tea a year, most of that tea—about 925,000 pounds of it—was smuggled from Holland. The bulk of tea sales happened on the black market because the majority of colonists refused to buy tea from the British. Buying British tea meant paying a tax that the colonists felt was unfair so long as they were denied a vote in Parliament: No taxation without representation! When the Townshend Acts imposed a tax on tea in 1767, Americans turned to smugglers, paying a premium to avoid the detested tax while still drinking tea. Even after Parliament repealed most of the Townshend Acts in 1770, it left in place the tax on tea.

Hoping to discourage the colonists from buying tea from anyone else, Parliament passed the Tea Act in May 1773. The new law granted the East India Company the complete monopoly on tea exportation to the colonies and even excused the Company from paying the usual export taxes to the government. Instead, the colonists would pay the import tax, small though it was. To make sure the Company had the money it needed to go ahead with this venture, the Bank of England lent it an additional 1.4 million pounds. So it wasn't only a tea exporter that had a lot at stake in getting the colonies to buy tea; it was also the British government and the Bank of England! The East India

This political cartoon of 1775 depicts King George III and Lord Mansfield, a prominent member of Parliament, driving two horses labeled "Obstinacy" and "Pride" into an abyss that represents the war with the American colonies.

Company had become the first "too big to fail" corporation in the world. If it collapsed, the cost to Britain would be enormous. It would be a very bitter cup for the king to swallow!

The concessions to the Company were meant to prop up a failing business and, at the same time, prove that Parliament had the right to tax the colonies. Some government ministers suggested that the British export tax be kept while the import tax on the colonies be dropped. However, Lord Frederick North, the prime minister, considered this a brilliant opportunity to prove that the Americans would swallow a tax so long as it was in their own economic interest. He felt sure the colonists wouldn't object because the import tax was so low, a mere threepence per pound, which guaranteed a much lower total cost than what the tea smugglers charged for their inferior product (since now there would be no export tax cost added to the East India Company tea). The British Crown insisted it was actually doing the colonies a favor, offering them high-quality tea at a lower price—so long as they bought from the monopoly favored by the government, the East India Company. If that price included a small tax, what difference should that make?

"Men," Lord North wrote, "will always go to the cheapest markets."

King George III, at the time of his coronation in 1761.

The Sons of Liberty

In 1765, a secret group called the Loyal Nine formed in response to British tyranny, especially to protest the Stamp Act. This small group soon grew into the Sons of Liberty, with branches in every colony. Its members were mostly middle-class merchants and lawyers and local politicians. They used newspapers and printed sheets called "broadsides" to encourage the public to support democratic rule in the colonies and to fight the imperious taxes. The Stamp Act meant that every piece of paper, including even playing cards, had to carry an official revenue stamp showing that the tax had been paid. The Sons of Liberty organized boycotts of British goods in protest and successfully pressured Britain to drop the tax . . . only to see it replaced by the Townshend Acts, which faced similar boycotts until most of those acts were repealed. But the tax on tea was left in place.

Repeal or Funeral of Stamp Act, a British political cartoon from 1766, shows men in a funeral procession heading into a tomb while a dog lifts its leg on the leader of the group. The demise of the Stamp Act is shown as a mournful occasion, one of deep political failure. Parliament kept trying to tax the colonies but couldn't find a way to do it without disastrous results, as even a dog could sense.

This stamp showed that tax had been paid on paper goods—anything from a newspaper to playing cards to a last will and testament.

Anti–Stamp Act cartoon printed in the *Pennsylvania Journal* in 1765.

The Boston chapter of the Sons of Liberty was one of the most vocal and active. Its membership included names everyone thinks of when the topic is the American Revolution: Sam Adams, his cousin John Adams, John Hancock, and Paul Revere. Members of other chapters included Patrick Henry and Benedict Arnold. James Otis, another of Boston's Sons of Liberty, made popular the slogan that became the motto for the colonists: "Taxation without representation is tyranny." He first said it to protest that Parliament wasn't treating the colonists like British citizens but like lesser people. What the Sons of Liberty really feared was being treated like the Irish, a population controlled by London

with no say in their own government. According to the English Bill of Rights of 1689, the public—meaning men with property, of course, not women or the poor—had the right to vote for their representatives in the government. Since even the wealthiest colonists couldn't vote, they had no direct representation in Parliament. Why didn't King George III solve this whole mess by allowing the colonists to vote? Because he didn't feel they were truly English. They had become American. And indeed they had.

John Adams (after 1783), by an unknown artist.

Lord North obviously hadn't met the Sons of Liberty! They recognized that the price was actually far greater than three thin pennies (roughly a dollar today). It was admitting that Parliament could tax the colonies whenever and on whatever it wanted. And that the colonies had no say.

As Benjamin Franklin wrote to a friend, England believed "that threepence on a pound of tea, of which one does not drink perhaps ten pounds a year, is sufficient to overcome the patriotism of an American. . . . They have no idea that people can act from any principle but that of [self-] interest." In other words, the British government thought people would prefer cheaper tea, even if the price included a tax they thought was unfair.

The Sons of Liberty had tried to garner favor with the colonists against taxes in the past, but most folks remained uninterested—until the Tea Act. With it, Samuel Adams found a cause he could rally people around. They knew what was at stake. The colonists recognized the underhanded tactic of using cheap goods to sneak in a tax. And Franklin gave Adams plenty of ammunition. Somehow (probably from Thomas Pownall, a former governor of the Massachusetts Bay Colony), Franklin had acquired a group of letters written by the current governor, Thomas Hutchinson, to Thomas Whately, a British treasury bureaucrat, during the riots of 1768–69 over the Townshend Acts. In the letters, Hutchinson called on the British government to send troops to Boston to impose order and security over the dangerous mobs. Franklin advised that the letters should be made known only to the most responsible civic leaders. But the

Benjamin Franklin (1778),
by Joseph-Siffrede Duplessis.

Sam Adams (1772), a copy of a portrait
by John Singleton Copley.

threat of force, of treating the colonies like occupied territory, enraged Adams, who made copies of the letters in 1773 and sent them to every town in Massachusetts. The leaked information infuriated King George III. He saw it as more proof of how uncivilized the colonists were. The colonists, for their part, saw it as proof of how brutish the British government was. Word spread quickly, and burning Hutchinson in effigy became a popular sport. A petition to have Hutchinson removed as governor was on its way to London at the same time that seven ships loaded with East India Company tea were heading for the colonies. They probably crossed each other at sea.

The *Eleanor*, *Dartmouth*, *William*, and *Beaver* were bound for Boston.

The *Polly* sailed for Philadelphia.

The *Nancy* headed for New York.

The *London* was on its way to Charleston, South Carolina.

Before the ships arrived, word of their coming spread up and down the coast. First the colonies had to put up with brutish governors treating the colonists like criminals. Now they were having a bitter tea tax shoved down their throats!

The colonies were in an uproar. Broadsides papered the streets. It was the first warning that a revolution was about to start.

One notice posted on the Boston docks proclaimed: "The hour of destruction, or manly opposition, to the machinations of tyranny, stares you in the face." Which meant: Fight or prepare to be a servant to the Crown.

Burning a hated political figure in effigy was a popular way to express anger. In this 1794 image, an effigy of John Jay is burned. Jay was the American envoy to Great Britain who engineered a trade treaty with England. He was seen as a traitor by the American people.

THE STATE BLACKSMITHS
Forging fetters for the Americans

Published according to Act of Parliament 1st March 1776.

A political cartoon published in 1776 in London shows the English Parliament forging shackles to imprison the colonies. Lord Mansfield wields a hammer, and Lord North holds a lorgnette in one hand and, in the other, a paper that reads "An act for prohibiting all trade." Another lord works the bellows while yet another holds a small hammer in one hand and an anchor in the other. Looking through the window is King George III.

Broadsides

The broadsides were like public notice boards, and they warned people that Parliament was trying to enslave them by making them pay taxes without any fair representation in their own government. The language used was heated. Tea was called "that noxious brew, that baneful weed, that poisonous draught." In fact, to convince women not to buy and serve tea (since tea parties were especially popular gatherings for women), some people spread rumors about insects breeding in the tea. One woman was insulted by this sly tactic; she wanted to be told about the political, economic, and social reasons not to buy tea. She complained in a letter to the newspaper *Massachusetts Spy* on December 23, 1773:

If Tea has been really known to be a baneful weed, a poisonous draught, &c., why were not these arguments used against the use of it in former times, before it was thought a political evil?

There is no doubt but the abuse of this as well as of any other thing may be attended with bad consequences, but that it is evil in itself and in all cases is not proved from its having been sometimes used imprudently. . . . I imagine that if the gentlemen who are fully acquainted with all the political reasons for discarding the use of Tea were to publish a full and plain narrative of matters of fact, so that we might see how it comes to pass that the use of Tea is a political evil in this country, and instruct us in all they know about it, that it would be a much more probable method to make us leave off the use of it than the calling it hard names and telling us scarecrow stories about it.

　　　A WOMAN.

New-York May 30th 1770.

THE FEMALE PATRIOT, No. I.

ADDRESSED TO THE

TEA-DRINKING LADIES OF NEW-YORK.

WHEN ADAM first fell into SATAN's Snare,
　And forfeited his Bliss to please the Fair;
GOD from his Garden drove the sinful Man,
And thus the Source of human Woes began.
'Twas weak in ADAM, for to please his Wife,
To lose his access to the Tree of Life:
His dear bought Knowledge all his Sons deplore,
DEATH their Inheritance, and SIN their Store.
But why blame ADAM, since his Brainless Race
Will lose their ALL to obtain a beautious FACE;
And will their Honour, Pride, and Wealth lay down,
Rather then see a lovely Woman frown.
The Ladies are not quite so complisant,
If they want TEA, they'll storm and rave and rant,
And call their Lordly Husbands Ass and CLOWN,
The jest of Fools and Sport of all the Town.
A pleasant Story lately I heard told
Of MADAM HORNBLOOM, a noted Scold,
Last Day her Husband said, "My dearest Life,
My Kind, my Fair, my Angel of a Wife;
Just now, from LONDON, there's a Ship come in
Brings noble News will raise us Merchants Fame,
The Fruits of our non-importation Scheme.
The Parliament, dear Saint, may they be blest
Have great part of our Grievances redrest:"
"Have they indeed," replies the frowning Dame,
"Say, is there not some Tea and China come."
"Why, no! We can't import that Indian Weed,
That Duty's still a Rod above our Head."
"Curse on your Heads, you nasty fumbling Crew,
Then round his Shoulders the hard Broom-Stick flew,
Go, dirty CLOD-POLE! get me some Shushong,
This Evening I've invited MADAM STRONG.
--- Silence --- you BLOCKHEAD --- hear, the Lady
　　knocks!

The other colonies were watching, wondering what Boston would do as the ships neared that port first. One Philadelphia patriot sent a letter to the *Boston Gazette*: "All that we fear, is that you will shrink at Boston. . . . We fear that you will suffer this tea to be landed."

A New York handbill warned, "If you touch one grain of this accursed tea, you are undone. America is threatened with worse than Egyptian slavery." (This was a reference to the biblical story of the Egyptian pharaoh's enslavement of the Israelites.)

The four ships were closing in on Boston with their cargo of hundreds of chests of tea. In the days after that first broadside, rumors swirled through the streets. Everyone knew that four men had been chosen as tea "consignees," or agents, who would sell the detested tea for the East India Company and pocket a tidy profit of a 6 percent commission—at the expense of liberty.

The agents were chosen for their loyalty to the British Crown. They were Benjamin Faneuil Jr., a merchant; Richard Clarke, another merchant, who happened to be Governor Hutchinson's nephew; and, worst of all, the governor's own sons, Thomas Jr. and Elisha.

Early on the morning of November 2, the Sons of Liberty sent notes to all the tea agents, demanding that they appear at the Liberty Tree the next day at noon to resign their posts as tea consignees. "Fail not upon your peril," the note warned.

A growing group of restless patriots waited at the Liberty Tree. John Hancock was there. So were Sam Adams, Paul Revere, and Joseph Warren. The church bells rang out noon . . . then one o'clock . . . then two o'clock. A murmur rose through the crowd. The tea consignees weren't coming. Instead, they were holding their own secret meeting at Richard Clarke's warehouse.

Nine delegates hurried to Clarke's address. Rather than a calm discussion, a brawl broke out, with the tea agents and their men against the furious Sons of Liberty. Windows and doors were broken, noses bloodied, and eyes blackened. But the agents insisted they had a right to sell the tea.

Outraged, Adams called for a meeting a couple of days later at Faneuil Hall. So many people came, they couldn't all fit in the building. The decision was clear: No matter what the tea agents said, no tea would land in Boston. Or else!

But the tea consignees still refused to listen. Now all of Boston bristled, like a growling dog. Each of the tea agents—except for Clarke—left the city until things cooled down. They were afraid of being tarred and feathered.

The Liberty Tree was located in Boston, at the corner of Orange and Essex Streets. The elm tree was a gathering place for colonists to protest against British rule. British soldiers cut it down in 1775.

Tarring and Feathering

Tarring and feathering is an old European form of punishment. It first appeared in the colonies in direct response to British authority. John Gilchrist, a merchant in Norfolk, Virginia, suspected that his smuggling activities had been reported by Captain William Smith in the spring of 1766. As a punishment and deterrent for any further interference, Gilchrist, along with some friends (including the mayor of Norfolk), grabbed Smith, painted tar on his body, threw feathers on his tarred skin, and paraded the unfortunate man through the town. The Virginians had started a trend that would be eagerly adopted by their fellow colonists. There are records of thirteen incidents of tarring and feathering by the spring of 1770, all inflicted on customs or tax officials (or snitches spying for them). Massachusetts had the most, eight, followed by New York, with two, and one each in Connecticut, Virginia, and Pennsylvania. The punishment became an act of political and economic resistance, so much so that the group of men in Philadelphia who organized to protest the tea tax called themselves the Committee for Tarring and Feathering.

Bostonians tarring and feathering a taxman. The act was meant to humiliate the recipient and rarely caused permanent damage, as the material used was sticky pine tar, not hot tar.

Into this tense atmosphere, the first tea ship arrived at Griffin's Wharf on November 28. The *Dartmouth* was filled with 114 chests of the dreaded tea.

Sam Adams called for a meeting the next day at Faneuil Hall, but there was such a big crowd, with people coming from neighboring towns, they couldn't all fit. Instead, the gathering was moved to Old South Meeting House. More than five thousand colonists packed the space. Once again, the vote was unanimous—the tea would *not* be unloaded. No duties would be paid on it. Period. The ships and their tea would be sent straight back to England.

The tea consignees were given until three o'clock to respond.

Their answer was to leave the city again.

But that wasn't a solution for Sam Adams and the Sons of Liberty. If the merchants didn't refuse the tea—if they simply left it on board—then the king's customs agents would seize the cargo, giving the consignees twenty days to claim it and pay the tax. If the consignees didn't pay the tax, then the customs agents would auction off the tea and pay the tax with the proceeds. But the colonists were adamant: No tax could be paid by anyone, no matter what! The *Dartmouth*—tea included—had to

Faneuil Hall, Boston.

be turned back to England before the twenty days were up.

The clock was ticking as two more tea ships arrived at Griffin's Wharf. The *Eleanor* landed on December 3, and the *Beaver* followed four days later. (The *William* ran aground on Cape Cod and never reached Boston.) British soldiers guarded the ships—and their cargo totaling 340 chests of tea—while rumors raced around town. Some claimed that the British were lining up the huge cannon on their warships at nearby Castle Island to fire on the wharf and any protesters. Others remembered the Whately letters and feared that the redcoats were preparing an attack on the entire city.

⁂

The twenty days were almost up. The tea would be taxed without the tea agents or shipowners doing anything. And now, even if the shipowners wanted to leave, the governor had ordered them to stay. The ships would be held in port until they could off-load their goods and pay the detested taxes.

Sam Adams called one last meeting at the Old South Meeting House, on December 16. It drew the biggest crowd of all, with the mood as dark and cloudy as the rainy skies. Adams called for calm and sent a delegation to Governor Hutchinson himself this time, demanding that he let the tea ships leave.

The Green Dragon Tavern in Boston's North End, where the Sons of Liberty planned the Tea Party, as sketched by John Johnston, one of the men involved.

This engraving by Paul Revere depicts British ships landing in Boston, bringing troops to enforce order on the rebellious colonists.

The governor, at least, was still in Boston. He hadn't run away like the tea agents. He said he'd give the Sons of Liberty his answer at 5:00 P.M.

But when the men returned for his response, the house was empty! Hutchinson had fled like the other British cowards. And that was his answer.

Back at the meeting, John Hancock, John Adams, and Paul Revere gave patriotic speeches.

They told stories of support, like the people in Lexington who'd made a public bonfire of all their tea, cleaning out their shops and cupboards. When the report came back of Hutchinson's escape, Sam Adams proclaimed loudly, "This meeting can do nothing more to save this country!"

And that was the signal.

About a hundred young men and boys,

organized into three groups under commanders, headed to the wharf. Peter Slater was the youngest participant in the Boston Tea Party, at age thirteen, but there were fifteen other teenagers, and most of the rest were in their twenties. The majority were of English ancestry, but Irish, Scottish, French, Portuguese, and African men also joined in. Thousands more watched and protected the Tea Partyers in a massive demonstration of public support for the colonies' right to democratic rule.

The men and boys smudged their faces with coal and soot and wrapped themselves in blankets as a crude disguise. The Sons of Liberty wanted them to look like proud Mohawk Indians. Nobody could have mistaken them for real Mohawks, but they were definitely proud!

They strode quickly, lanterns and torches lit in the cold night, the moon a thin new sliver in the star-spangled sky. This was no rowdy mob. None of them had weapons. The British warships loomed over them all, but no one challenged them. The captains of the *Eleanor*, *Dartmouth*, and *Beaver* all hid in their cabins and let the "Mohawks" go about their work.

The Boston Tea Party.

Everyone was careful not to harm the ships in any way. A padlock was broken—and quickly replaced. The colonists wanted to make clear to the British that this wasn't an unruly mob of rioters but Americans demonstrating for their rights.

For the next three hours, the groups worked steadily, hauling up the heavy chests, breaking them open, and throwing the tea into the harbor. Mountains of tea rose in the water, so high that they towered over the ships. Some fellows got into rowboats and poked at the piles, trying to sink the leaves, but there was simply too much of the stuff.

What about the *William*, the ship that had run aground on December 10? It was stranded, not lost at sea, so the British could save the precious tea. And in fact they did. The captain, Joseph Loring, managed to unload fifty-eight chests of tea before abandoning the ship. Who helped him? None other than Jonathan Clarke, the son of Richard Clarke, one of Boston's tea agents. He sent the chests to Boston, directly into the hands of his father—all except two cases, which were directed to Jonathan Clarke's cousin David Greenough to sell on Cape Cod. Some of that tea was sold to Colonel Willard Knowles of Eastham, the gentleman in charge of his town's stock of ammunition. Rumors flew quickly about the role the two men played in

harboring the "evil tea." Talk became action in March, when a group of eighty men tried to "wrest the Towns Ammunition out of the Hands of Col. Knowles," now regarded as an untrustworthy citizen. After all, if Knowles had hidden British tea, how could he be trusted to guard the militia's supplies? To prove his patriotism, Knowles destroyed the tea, pleading for forgiveness. The townspeople must have believed him, because he was allowed to stay in charge of the ammunition depot. Greenough, seeing Knowles's rough treatment, got rid of his tea, too. If he hadn't, he knew his neighbors would never speak to him again.

The type of tea chest used by the East India Company to import tea from China into the American colonies.

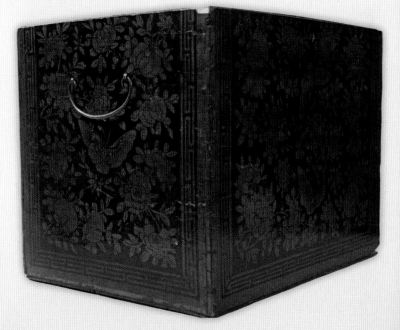

That still left fifty-six chests of tea in Richard Clarke's Boston warehouse. In March, the Sons of Liberty followed the trail from the *William* straight to the storerooms, but they discovered only twenty-eight cases. They carried all the chests to the harbor, where they smashed each one and threw the tea into the water. Not satisfied until they uncovered every leaf that hadn't already been drunk by the British stationed in their town, they hunted for the rest, tracking down the last sixteen chests at the Boston tea shop of Davison, Newman, & Company. On March 7, 1774, a group of about sixty patriots, dressed again like Mohawks, made one last giant cup of tea in the harbor, in the second Boston Tea Party. Richard Clarke may have paid the tax on this tea, but no American drank any.

The day after Boston's first Tea Party, Sam Adams got up early to send messages to the Sons of Liberty in New York and Philadelphia. From there, the news spread throughout the colonies. Adams wrote:

> *Every ounce of tea on board was immersed in the Bay, without the least injury to private property. The Spirit of the People on this occasion surprised all parties who viewed the Scene. We conceived it our duty to afford you the most early advice of this interesting event by express. Which departing immediately obliges us to conclude.*

The "express" was Paul Revere, riding on horseback with the news. He reached New York on December 21, and Philadelphia three days later. He was back in Boston by the day after Christmas with the news of how the church bells rang and

Paul Revere (1768–70), by John Singleton Copley.

crowds cheered when they heard about the doings in Boston.

The other colonies applauded, too, when they heard. And inspired by Boston's example, they had their own tea parties.

In Philadelphia, thousands had come to a meeting about the tea and voted for eight resolutions, asserting the right of the colonies not to be taxed without representation and demanding that the arriving tea be returned to England. Led by Dr. Benjamin Rush, Colonel William Bradford, and other Sons of Liberty, the meeting was held in the Pennsylvania State House (now Independence Hall). The most important resolutions were:

✳ That the duty imposed by Parliament upon tea landed in America is a tax on the Americans, or levying contributions on them without their consent.

✳ That the resolution lately entered into by the East India Company, to send out their tea to America subject to the payment of duties [taxes] on its being landed here, is

A view of Philadelphia's waterfront and a map of Philadelphia (1768).

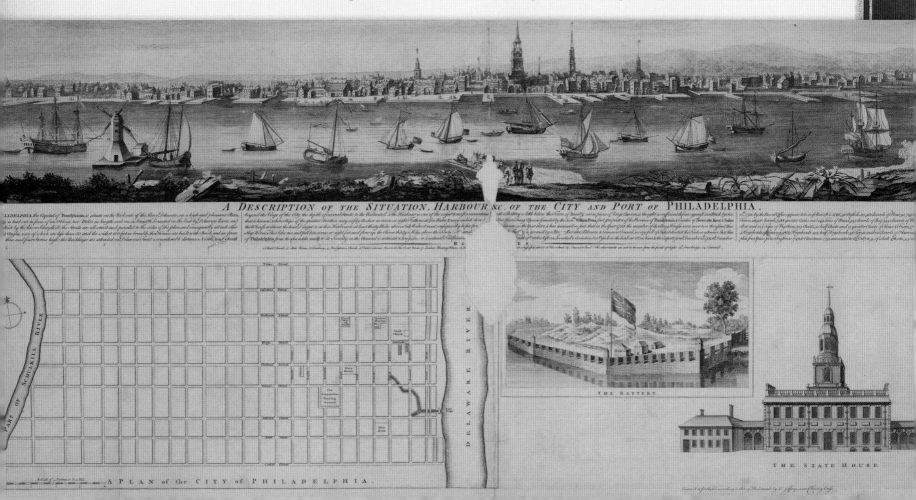

The Philadelphia State House was the meeting place where resolutions were passed on how to deal with the tea.

an open attempt to enforce the ministerial plan, and a violent attack upon the liberties of America.

All the resolutions were printed in the *Pennsylvania Gazette* on October 16, 1773, and became the first public protest against importing taxed tea from Britain. In fact, the language from the Philadelphia meeting was incorporated into Boston's response the next month and adopted in the meeting at Faneuil Hall in December. So although

Philadelphia's tea party came after Boston's, the arguments against the tea tax arose first in the home of the Liberty Bell.

The Philadelphia Sons of Liberty and the local Committee for Tarring and Feathering posted handbills threatening the captain and Delaware River pilots with the American punishment of tar and feathers if they dared to bring the tea ship to the city. By the end of November, there was so much anger that two of the tea agents, Abel James and Henry Drinker, were convinced that the tea could

TO THE
Delaware Pilots.

WE took the Pleasure, some Days since, of kindly admonishing you *to do your Duty*, if perchance you should meet with the (*Tea*,) SHIP POLLY, CAPTAIN AYRES, a THREE DECKER which is hourly expected.

We have now to add, that Matters ripen fast here; and that *much is expected from those Lads who meet with the Tea Ship.*----There is some Talk of A HANDSOME REWARD FOR THE PILOT WHO GIVES THE FIRST GOOD ACCOUNT OF HER.----How that may be, we cannot *for certain* determine: But ALL agree, that TAR and FEATHERS will be his Portion, who pilots her into this Harbour. And we will answer for ourselves, that, whoever is committed to us, as an Offender against the Rights of *America*, will experience the utmost Exertion of our Abilities; as

THE COMMITTEE FOR TARRING AND FEATHERING.

P. S. We expect you will furnish yourselves with Copies of the foregoing and following Letter; which are printed for this Purpose, that the Pilot who meets with Captain *Ayres* may favor him with a Sight of them.

Committee of Taring and Feathering.

TO
Capt. AYRES,

Of the SHIP *POLLY*, on a Voyage from *London* to *Philadelphia*.

SIR,

WE are informed that you have, imprudently, taken Charge of a Quantity of Tea; which has been sent out by the *India* Company, *under the Auspices of the Ministry,* as a Trial of *American* Virtue and Resolution.

Now, as your Cargo, on your Arrival here, will most assuredly bring you into hot water; and as you are perhaps a Stranger *to these Parts*, we have concluded to advise you of the present Situation of Affairs in *Philadelphia*----that, taking Time by the Forelock, you may stop short in your dangerous Errand----secure your Ship against the Rafts of combustible Matter which may be set on Fire, and turned loose against her; and more than all this, that you may preserve your own Person, from the Pitch and Feathers that are prepared for you.

In the first Place, we must tell you, that the *Pennsylvanians* are, *to a Man*, passionately fond of Freedom; the Birthright of *Americans*; and at all Events are determined to enjoy it.

That they sincerely believe, no Power on the Face of the Earth has a Right to tax them without their Consent.

That in their Opinion, the Tea in your Custody is designed by the Ministry to enforce such a Tax, which they will undoubtedly oppose; and in so doing, give you every possible Obstruction.

We are nominated to a very disagreeable, but necessary Service.--- To our Care are committed all Offenders against the Rights of *America*; and hapless is he, whose evil Destiny has doomed him to suffer at our Hands.

You are sent out on a diabolical Service; and if you are so foolish and obstinate as to compleat your Voyage; by bringing your Ship to Anchor in this Port, you may run such a Gauntlet, as will induce you, in your last Moments, most heartily to curse those who have made you the Dupe of their Avarice and Ambition.

What think you Captain, of a Halter around your Neck----ten Gallons of liquid Tar decanted on your Pate----with the Feathers of a dozen wild Geese laid over that to enliven your Appearance?

Only think seriously of this----and fly to the Place from whence you came----fly without Hesitation---- without the Formality of a Protest----and above all, Captain *Ayres* let us advise you to fly without the wild Geese Feathers.

Your Friends *to serve*

Philadelphia, Nov. 27, 1773. THE COMMITTEE *as before subscribed*

not safely land. (Or, really, that *they* wouldn't be safe if it landed.) When news came of the Boston Tea Party, the popular leaders felt strengthened in their resolve to return the tea untouched. By the time the tea ship *Polly*, with its 697 chests of tea, had arrived downriver from Philadelphia at Chester on December 25, Gilbert Barkley, another tea agent who had been aboard the ship, got off and resigned his commission, afraid to sell any tea. Scouts were sent out to spot the ship and keep it from docking. As one broadside declared: "Captain Ayres . . . ought to have known our people better than to have expected we would be so mean as to suffer his rotten tea to be funneled down our throats with the Parliament's duty mixed with it."

Monday Morning, December 27, 1773.

THE Tea-Ship being arrived, every Inhabitant who wishes to preserve the Liberty of America, is desired to meet at the STATE-HOUSE, This Morning, precisely at TEN o'Clock, to advise what is best to be done on this alarming Crisis.

Broadside, tea ship arrival, Philadelphia, 1773.

But Ayres didn't know better. He continued to sail up the Delaware River, until the ship was stopped at the Arch Street Wharf. Several gentlemen from the Committee for Tarring and Feathering escorted the terrified captain into Philadelphia. Despite the broadside threats, he was treated politely and given comfortable rooms in William Bradford's London Coffee House (coffee, of course, not tea). Two days later, a meeting was called in the State House yard to decide what to do with the captain and his ship. More than eight thousand Philadelphians showed up, making this the largest assembly yet held in the colonies.

Captain Ayres listened nervously as a series of resolutions were adopted. The first was "that the tea . . . shall not be landed." Not only was the tea refused, but so was all the cargo, and the captain was ordered to leave as soon as he had provisioned the ship for the long journey back to England.

Another broadside threatened to tar and feather the tea agents and any river pilot who tried to help the *Polly* dock. Despite the violent words,

London Coffee House, on the southwest corner of Market and Front Streets, Philadelphia. Watercolor by Benjamin Ridgeway Evans.

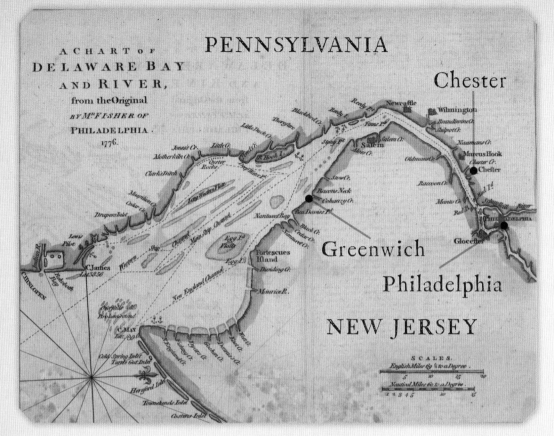

Map of Delaware Bay and the Delaware River.

altogether. Instead, she landed in the Delaware Bay, at Greenwich, New Jersey. This was on December 12, 1774, and Captain Allen figured that the tea could travel secretly overland the rest of the way. When word got out that tea had been on the ship and off-loaded into a pro-British Loyalist's home near the wharf, a group of young men, following the Boston example, dressed as Indians, carried torches, and "liberated" the tea on December 22. They lugged the heavy chests to the village green, broke them open, and burned all the tea in a large bonfire. The East India Company, using its agents housed in Philadelphia, sued the men they named as Indians for destroying their property. They said that Richard Howell (later a governor of New Jersey), Ebenezer Elmer (later a member of the House of Representatives), Silas Newcomb (later a brigadier general of the New Jersey militia), and Ephraim Newcomb (Silas's son, later a prominent doctor) all owed 1,200 pounds in damages. The men, a distinguished group, were arrested, but the trial was delayed until after the Battles of Lexington and Concord, Massachusetts,

the actual situation was calm, though direct. Captain Ayres was taken back to his ship and politely invited to leave.

The captain got the message. He couldn't wait to get out to sea. As quickly as he could, he loaded food and water into his ship and left, taking all the tea back with him.

Because of this fiery welcome, the following year a smaller tea ship, the *Greyhound*, decided to avoid sailing up the Delaware River to Philadelphia

View of Charleston, looking across the Cooper River.

in April 1775. By then, the American Revolution had started in earnest, and a sympathetic jury refused to convict these prominent townsfolk.

The *London*, one of the original group of seven tea ships, landed in Charleston Harbor on December 1, 1773, with 257 chests of tea. That made Charleston the second city—after Boston—to receive a tea ship. The public was already wary, having read in the *South-Carolina Gazette* that the tea would allow Parliament to "raise a revenue, out of your pockets, against your consent, and to render assemblies of your representatives totally useless." Another writer in the newspaper warned that soon Parliament would tax colonists for the very "light of heaven."

Christopher Gadsden, a member of the South Carolina General Assembly and one of the most vocal Sons of Liberty, called a meeting to deal with the issue. Handbills urged people to come, as did the *Gazette*, saying the meeting was for those "who thought it would be criminal tamely to give up any of our essential rights as British subjects, and involve our posterity in a state little better than slavery." Many of the local merchants stayed away, more concerned with profit, as Lord North had predicted, and Gadsden opened the session by haranguing them for not coming. At least the tea consignees came once they were sent for, and they agreed to refuse the tea shipments.

Gadsden feared, however, that the governor, Lord Charles Greville Montagu, would simply take the tea and sell it himself, so the next step was to get all the town's merchants—the same people who hadn't come to the meeting—to promise not to buy the tea. When the merchants insisted that there was nothing that mattered more than profit, Gadsden argued back. As a businessman himself, he told them he understood their financial pain but declared that some things were more important than money.

What could that be? the merchants demanded.

"Freedom!" answered Gadsden.

Even before the tea tax, he had organized

Christopher Gadsden (1870), by Thomas Addis Emmet.

boycotts of British goods. Thanks to his efforts, the women of Charleston wore homespun clothes and carried homemade "liberty umbrellas" instead of the usual imported parasols. Now Gadsden convinced the merchants to promise that as long as they could sell the tea they already had in their shops, they wouldn't stock any more.

With the market for tea firmly closed, the *London* sat heavy in Charleston Harbor, its tea unloaded for three long weeks. The captain,

Alexander Curling, was warned that if he didn't leave with his unwanted cargo, his ship would be burned. In the meantime, Boston and Philadelphia dealt with their 1,037 chests of tea.

Lieutenant Governor William Bull, eager to avoid any confrontation with the stubborn Gadsden, ordered most of the tea secretly unloaded early in the morning of December 22 and locked the chests in the basement of the Old Exchange building. He thought he'd be able to sell the tea later, when tempers cooled. But they only got hotter—so hot that by the time the tea was finally sold, the American Revolution was in full swing and the profits, rather than going into Parliament's coffers as a tax, helped pay for the war against Britain. Not at all what the lieutenant governor had intended. The rest of the tea on board the *London*, a mere eighteen chests, headed on to New York, with hopes of a warmer—or rather, less heated—welcome.

When Sam Adams heard that the tea in Charleston had been unloaded, even though no tax had been paid, he wrote a sharp rebuke, saying that Boston had hoped for united opposition. "How great then was our chagrin to hear that through some internal division the grand cause was neglected.... Must then the liberties of the present and future ages be sacrificed to some unhappy feuds in Carolina?" If Carolina didn't stand with her sister colonies, what hope was there? Adams urged "that by uniting we stand and by dividing we fall."

Gadsden realized to his horror that Charleston had been the only colony to allow the cursed tea to be unloaded. It was a small consolation that it hadn't been taxed or sold. Not only that,

View of New York Harbor.

but Charleston merchants were still selling tea—admittedly, tea that was already in stock—unlike the other cities, where all tea was being boycotted. Gadsden himself became a devoted coffee drinker.

Of the original seven, the only ships now bound for New York were the *London*, rerouted from Charleston, and the *Nancy*, which had been delayed by storms.

As soon as word that the tea was on its way reached New York, the Sons of Liberty called for a meeting, just as in the other colonies. On November 29, 1773, the townspeople agreed that anyone who helped bring in taxed tea would be considered an enemy of the liberties of America: "We will not deal with, or employ, or have any connection with him." Whether the tax was paid in Britain or in America, "our liberties are equally affected."

The merchants who had been chosen as tea agents read the way the wind blew. They reported to Governor William Tryon that they would not accept the tea. The governor and his council decided they

This engraving, *New York Agitation Against Tea*, depicts a heated discussion by the Sons of Liberty on how to handle the tea and any who helped land it.

would allow the tea to land, but only so they could store it in military barracks until a decision was made on how to deal with it.

Isaac Sears, John Lamb, and Alexander McDougall, the leading Sons of Liberty in New York, called another meeting on December 17, reading letters from Boston and Philadelphia outlining their decisions to turn back the tea. The mayor presented the governor's offer to store the tea in the fort while waiting to hear what England wanted, but the temperature at the meeting had risen, and shouts of support for Boston and Philadelphia made it clear that no tea would be allowed to land. Why wait to hear what Parliament wanted? What mattered was what the Americans wanted—no, demanded!

City Hall, Wall Street, New York City.

At the very moment the meeting was taking place, Paul Revere was on his way to New York with the news of the Boston Tea Party. When he arrived a few days later, the New York Sons of Liberty knew what they had to do: the same as Boston! The governor backed down in the face of so much anger and agreed that he would not use force to land the tea. Instead, he would follow the will of the citizens. A wise decision, if he didn't want to be tarred and feathered himself.

But no tea came. Prepared to have their own tea party, the New York Sons of Liberty had to wait until the following year for their chance. Because of bad weather, the tea ship *Nancy*, carrying 698 chests of tea, did not reach Sandy Hook, New Jersey, until April 18, 1774. The *New York Journal* reported:

Ever since her departure from Europe, she has met with a continued succession of misfortune, having on board something worse than a Jonah, which, after being tossed in the tempestuous ocean, it is hoped, like him, will be thrown back upon the place from whence it came.

To the Public.

THE long expected TEA SHIP arrived laſt night at Sandy-Hook, but the pilot would not bring up the Captain till the ſenſe of the city was known. The committee were immediately informed of her arrival, and that the Captain ſolicits for liberty to come up to provide neceſſaries for his return. The ſhip to remain at Sandy-Hook. The committee conceiving it to be the ſenſe of the city that he ſhould have ſuch liberty, ſignified it to the Gentleman who is to ſupply him with proviſions, and other neceſſaries. Advice of this was immediately diſpatched to the Captain; and whenever he comes up, care will be taken that he does not enter at the cuſtomhouſe, and that no time be loſt in diſpatching him.

New-York, April 19, 1774.

Once the ship was moored in Sandy Hook, a regular stop for shipping traffic coming to New York, local pilots refused to escort the *Nancy* or her captain, Benjamin Lockyer, into New York Harbor. The crew members were all stuck there. And to make it clear they'd stay, a committee of the Sons of Liberty boarded the *Nancy*. They had to prevent the crew from leaving so there would be the full complement of sailors needed to sail the ship home right away. So the colonists chained and locked up the small boats on board. That way nobody could get to shore, though some desperate sailors built a small raft and tried to float away, only to be stopped by the alert Sons of Liberty. The colonists warned Captain Lockyer that "for the safety of your cargo, your vessel, and your persons, it will be most prudent for you to return" to England. They escorted him into the city to get supplies needed for the trip back. He was also taken to see the tea agent Henry White, who refused the tea but was not permitted to go to the Custom House in case he felt the urge to pay some tax. And where did they put up this fine captain while waiting for him to reprovision? In the Coffee House on Wall Street. (Again, coffee, not tea. The symbolism was probably clear to the captain.)

Meanwhile, the other tea ship from Charleston, the *London*, now under the command of Captain Chambers, arrived on April 22, 1774. The New York Sons of Liberty had heard from the Charleston Sons of Liberty that there were eighteen chests of tea hidden on board. The captain insisted there weren't, and he showed the *London*'s cargo list as proof; however, a quick search revealed his

Raising the Liberty Pole. Liberty poles were often erected in town squares as well as on private property both before and during the American Revolution. They would often be torn down by British authorities, only to be re-erected by the Sons of Liberty and others.

lie—and the tea. Fumbling for an excuse, the captain claimed the tea as his personal property and hence not part of the ship's cargo. The committee, shipowners, and captain all went to Fraunces Tavern to discuss what to do with both the tea and the ship. The townsfolk, however, wanted a quicker resolution, and a group of men boarded the ship that evening, found the cases, broke them open, and threw the tea into the river. They were careful not to touch the rest of the cargo. The splintered chests were used to stoke bonfires in the streets while the men celebrated their victory over greed and unjust taxation.

Although the tea dumping had been calm enough, the men now turned to the *London*'s captain, furious at his lies. Luckily for him, he managed to escape a brutal beating, running to hide on the *Nancy*.

One New York newspaper noted, "No disguise of any kind was adopted or worn to shelter the person of those who participated in the work from observation or identification. It was a work which the public weal required, and it was done openly by the parties interested, and in the presence of all who saw fit to witness it." In other words, the men were proud to dump the tea since they were doing something for the public good, not committing any kind of crime. No matter what Parliament said.

A few days later, the *Nancy*—with both captains and all her unloaded cargo—left for Europe. Her departure was marked with a great ringing of bells, and the ships in the harbor raised their flags in a show of triumph. The Liberty pole was decorated and a salute was fired, in a city full of festive celebration.

※

When King George III received news of the Boston Tea Party, he became enraged. So did Parliament, which quickly passed the Boston Port Act as punishment, closing the city to all sea traffic until the destroyed tea was paid for. Boston was placed under martial law, effectively occupied by the British army, with nobody allowed to leave or enter without its permission.

The other colonies smuggled in goods in support of their Boston brethren. Still stung that Charleston had allowed some tea on her soil, Gadsden personally organized food to be shipped to Boston. He no longer said "Mother England." Instead, he called the country "our mother *in*

The Liberty Pole

Boston had its Liberty Tree, an old elm near Boston Common, where the Sons of Liberty often held meetings. New York had the Liberty pole, planted in public squares before and during the Revolution as a symbol of freedom. It was a tall wooden pole, stuck upright into the ground with a flag or cap on top. The cap idea came from the Phrygian cap, a soft, red, elfish-looking kind of hat worn by the ancient Greeks as a banner of liberty from the Romans. That's why a Phrygian cap graces the Seal of the U.S. Senate.

law"—a change in title that wasn't meant as a compliment. The tea parties and Britain's punishment of Boston solidified his resolve, as they did for many in the colonies. If the colonists had thought before that they were British subjects, with British rights, the tea tax and tea parties made them feel solidly American.

In response to the heavy British fist, the First Continental Congress met in Philadelphia later that year, on September 5, 1774. Gadsden came as South Carolina's representative. He went on to lead the First South Carolina Regiment in the Revolution and became brigadier general of that state's military forces. He's not remembered today for allowing tea to land in Charleston but for developing the flag design for the newborn U.S. Navy: a coiled rattlesnake ready to strike on a yellow banner with the words "Don't Tread on Me" inscribed below.

Those words became the rallying call for many other tea parties as the colonists felt more and more clearly their newly minted identity as Americans. All through the colonies, tea was no longer drunk. Coffee was the patriotic choice. Any chests of tea that arrived were burned or thrown into the water as smaller tea parties rippled up and down the coast for the next couple of years.

The rest, as they say, is history.

"Don't Tread on Me" flag, as originally designed by Christopher Gadsden.

Author's Note

The seven tea ships and the tea parties they

inspired were only the beginning. All up and down the thirteen colonies, groups both large and small imitated the original daring of the Sons of Liberty with their own impromptu tea revolts. Furious at Parliament's draconian punishment of Boston, the Americans focused their anger on the cause of all the problems: tea and the nefarious tax it carried. Thanks to the Boston Sons of Liberty, tea had become the most visible symbol of British oppression.

What price does a moral standard have, after all? Today, we might ask if we would rather buy cheap clothes made by people who are paid terrible wages, working in horrible conditions, or spend a little more for goods that are made under fair conditions. What would people value today? A cleaner environment? Better conditions for workers? What principles are worth paying for? The colonists thought their independence was worth that kind of price.

What exactly was Parliament's response to the tea dumping? The first news came to London with the arrival of the *Hayley*, on January 19, 1774, which happened to have Boston newspapers on board. Ironically, John Hancock owned the *Hayley*, so it was an American patriot who first got the word to London of the work done by the Sons of Liberty. On January 22, the stories from the Boston press were splashed all over the *St. James's Chronicle*. The news was confirmed by the *Polly*, back in port on January 25 with her original cargo undelivered. By the end of the month, all London had heard of the ruinous destruction of thousands of pounds' worth of property.

The king's ministers demanded an explanation from an influential American who had represented various colonial interests in Britain for most of the past two decades: Benjamin Franklin. Called to meet with the Privy Council in Whitehall on January 29, Franklin thought the session would be about the recently presented petition to have Hutchinson removed as governor of Boston, all the more necessary in the wake of the recent events there. He walked into the most crowded Privy Council meeting in memory. (Usually only a few nobles showed up on such occasions.) For this very public inquiry into the crimes of the colonies, thirty-six nobles came, all in their most impressive finery, seated around one very long table. The king's residence, St. James's Palace, could be seen

After the Tea Party, British troops occupied Boston with the intent of cutting the city off from all trade until the colonists paid for the destroyed tea.

through the windows, a reminder of who really called the shots.

Besides the lords, the seats were filled with politicians, some of them British allies of Franklin, such as the scientist Joseph Priestley and Edmund Burke, the Irish orator and member of Parliament. But most were sneering enemies, eager to see how Franklin would defend his homeland and his own actions in making public the private letters sent by Governor Hutchinson to the British government. The prime minister, Lord North, arrived late and found himself without a place to sit, standing instead next to the council president's chair. Franklin stood as well, one arm leaning on the mantel of the fireplace; "the muscles of his face had been previously composed, so as to afford a tranquil expression."

But that was the only bit of serenity in the entire proceeding. For nearly an hour, Solicitor General Alexander Wedderburn accused Franklin of leaking the Whately letters out of naked ambition, eager to get the governorship for himself. Given the latest news—the Boston Tea Party—it was clear that the colonies needed a stronger hand from Britain, not a weaker one. Wedderburn finished his summation with an image of Boston governed by Bostonians as a "tyranny greater than the Roman!" He considered the colonists to be imperial despots themselves, like the corrupt ancient Roman emperors, an image that's hard to square with Sam Adams or Paul Revere.

Franklin stood "the whole time like a rock, in the same posture, his head resting on his left hand, and in that attitude abiding the pelting of the pitiless storm." But inside he was seething. As he left the council chamber, he's said to have whispered to the solicitor general, "I will make your master a little king for this."

With Franklin silenced, Parliament first tried to charge with treason all those involved in dumping the tea into Boston Harbor. Without actual proof, however, that seemed a hard sell, even with Parliament as furious as it was. Instead, Lord North and King George III pushed through a series of brutal laws, called the Coercive Acts by the British and "the Intolerable Acts" by the Americans. It started with the Boston Port Act, which sealed off the harbor from all trade until the tea, tax included, had been paid for (which never happened due to the interruption of the Revolution). Then the charter granted by the Crown in 1691 for government in Massachusetts was replaced with a new act that guaranteed British control in the most heavy-handed way. From then on, town meetings could be held only with the governor's permission. Furthermore, the governor's council, all local officials, and judges would be appointed by the governor and paid only from the proceeds of customs or importation taxes (for example, the tax on tea).

The Administration of Justice Act guaranteed that any British official or soldier charged with a capital crime in America would be sent to England or to another colony for trial. Colonies could not control justice within their own borders anymore. Finally, the Quartering Act allowed the British to dispatch four regiments to Boston and house them in the homes of private citizens.

Not everyone in Parliament voted for these measures. Edmund Burke warned that the Crown should "reflect on how you are to govern a people who think they ought to be free and think they are not." Former prime minister William Pitt thought the punishments too harsh, imposed on the many innocent as well as the few actually guilty of destruction of property. Besides, he agreed with the colonists that "this country [England] has no right under heaven" to tax them.

Their voices were in the minority, however, with most ministers supporting Lord North's assessment: "We must control them or submit to them."

But the colonies were in no mood to be controlled.

In late January 1774, Princeton college students broke into the college's storerooms, intent on liberating the tea there. One student, Charles Beatty, described how they "gathered all the steward's winter store of tea and having made a fire on the campus we there burned near a dozen pound, tolled the bell, and made many spirited resolves." Their New Year's resolutions included burning an effigy of Governor Hutchinson, with a tea canister tied around its neck, in front of Nassau Hall. Not only did the students pledge to drink only coffee, but they gathered in large groups (three dozen or more) to call on known tea drinkers in town, confiscating any tea they found in the homes and burning it in the streets.

That spring, on May 23, the local chapter of the Sons of Liberty in Chestertown, Maryland, passed its own resolutions in response to the British troops occupying and sealing off Boston. Like the Princeton students, they agreed to ban all buying, selling, and drinking of tea shipped from England. Hearing that the newly arrived brig *Geddes* carried tea in its hold, the group boarded the ship and dumped all the tea into the Chester River. To this day, the city of Chestertown reenacts the Chestertown Tea Party every Memorial Day weekend.

A few months later, Thomas Charles Williams, a merchant from Annapolis, Maryland, working in London, tried to smuggle in nearly a ton of tea by hiding it in packages that were supposed to contain linen. When Richard Jackson, the captain of the ship, the *Peggy Stewart*, realized what was in the cases of linen, he was furious. Only a few years earlier, a customs officer in Annapolis had not allowed a ship to unload part of its cargo until the tax on all the contents had been paid. Given that British tea was now impossible to land in America without a fight, Jackson feared that his ship would be sent back to England with all of its original cargo. That would not only be an expensive proposition, but in this case, it could cost human lives—because most of the *Peggy Stewart*'s cargo was human: fifty-three indentured servants. Such servants had contracted to pay off their passage across the ocean with labor, working as much as seven, ten, or even fifteen years, after which they would be freed to find work wherever they could. If the ship had to turn back just as storm season began, the miserable servants might not survive a second, longer, more difficult journey.

Alerted by the captain to the problem as soon as the ship arrived in Annapolis, Anthony Stewart, the shipowner, and Williams's brothers and business partners, Joseph and James Williams, felt forced to pay the entire customs tax so the people could leave the ship. They left the tea on board, however, to be sent back to England. That didn't satisfy the townsfolk, who were outraged that tax had been paid. Angry mobs led by Dr. Charles Warfield threatened to lynch the shipowner and the merchants and burn down their homes. To pacify the public, the merchants offered up the tea instead. That wasn't enough, Warfield insisted, calling instead to have the ship and all its contents burned to ashes. Having been warned of Warfield's intentions, on October 19, Stewart ran the *Peggy Stewart* aground himself and set her on fire, along with 2,320 pounds of tea, in what came to be known as the Annapolis Tea Party.

This was the last time the East India Company tried to export tea to the colonies. Instead,

The Burning of Peggy Stewart (1896), by Francis Blackwell Mayer.

the Company turned to Eastern markets, selling Indian-grown opium to the Chinese. When China resisted the growing importation of the drug, another war began: the First Opium War of 1839–42. Effectively taken over by the government in 1857 and dissolved in 1874, the East India Company had long-reaching, lasting effects on British colonies in the East. You can still see echoes of the Company's power in the East India Club, established in 1849 for officers of the company. Although the corporation no longer exists, the club still does, a private gentlemen's association centrally located in St. James's Square in London, next to the Naval and Military Club and the London Library. Members now come from the most prominent ranks of British society to enjoy the American Bar, named in honor of the U.S. military officers who stayed there in World War II. Benjamin Franklin and Sam Adams would have happily joined them there for a drink . . . of coffee.

Liberty Triumphant. This cartoon celebrates America's triumph over England, winning her independence from the British oppressor. The Native Americans represent the Spirit of Liberty and how the Sons of Liberty disguised themselves for the Tea Party. Boxes of the dreaded tea that sparked the conflict are shown in the lower left. The devil whispering into the king's ears demonstrates how wrong the Crown was in its policy toward America.

Timeline

❋ **Late September / early October 1773**—Tea ships of the East India Company, stocked with a total of 544,000 pounds of tea—about 2,000 chests of the stuff—set sail from England. The *Eleanor*, *Dartmouth*, *William*, and *Beaver* head for Boston; the *Nancy* sets out for New York; the *Polly* sails to Philadelphia; and the *London* goes to Charleston, South Carolina.

❋ **Early October 1773**—Colonists hear rumors about the arrival of the tea ships. They meet and make plans about how to handle the situation up and down the coast.

❋ **October 16, 1773**—Colonists in Philadelphia meet at the State House and pass a list of eight resolutions in response to the tea tax and imminent arrival of the tea ships. The resolutions affirm that Parliament has no right to tax the colonies, that all tea will be sent back, and that it is the duty of every American to oppose the landing of the tea and to fight against such unjust taxation.

❋ **October 16, 1773**—The Philadelphia Resolutions are published in the *Pennsylvania Gazette*.

❋ **November 2, 1773**—In Boston, the Sons of Liberty demand that all tea agents resign their positions the next day. When they refuse, a fight breaks out between the tea agents, along with their supporters, and the Sons of Liberty.

❋ **November 5, 1773**—Samuel Adams calls a meeting at Faneuil Hall to discuss what to do about the tea and the tea agents. A unanimous agreement is made not to allow any tea to be unloaded into the city.

❋ **November 27, 1773**—The Committee for Tarring and Feathering posts broadsides warning Captain Ayres, the captain of the *Polly*, not to land his tea in Philadelphia but instead to return home—or suffer the consequences.

❋ **November 28, 1773**—The first tea ship, the *Dartmouth*, arrives in Boston. Tax must be paid within twenty days or the customs agents will claim the goods, sell the tea at auction, and use the proceeds to pay the tax, keeping the rest for the king's coffers.

❋ **November 29, 1773**—Sam Adams calls for another meeting at Faneuil Hall. So many people show up that the meeting is moved to the Old South Meeting House. The tea agents flee the city to avoid facing the angry colonists.

❋ **November 29, 1773**—Sons of Liberty hold a meeting in New York. All present agree not to allow the tea to be unloaded or taxed and that anyone who helps with the tea should be considered an "enemy of the liberties of America."

❋ **December 1, 1773**—The *London* lands in Charleston Harbor.

❋ **December 3, 1773**—Christopher Gadsden and other Sons of Liberty hold a meeting in the Great Hall of Charleston's Old Exchange. The tea consignees come and agree to refuse the tea.

❋ **December 3, 1773**—The second tea ship heading to Boston, the *Eleanor*, arrives.

❋ **December 7, 1773**—The third tea ship, the *Beaver*, docks in Boston.

❋ **December 7, 1773**—More broadsides are posted near Philadelphia, warning Delaware River pilots that if they help guide the *Polly* to port, they will suffer the same dire fate as Captain Ayres (of being tarred and feathered).

❋ **December 10, 1773**—The fourth tea ship going to Boston, the *William*, is caught in a storm and runs aground in Provincetown, Massachusetts.

❋ **December 13, 1773**—A meeting protesting the Philadelphia Resolutions is called in Plymouth, Massachusetts. Worried about the possible "dangerous and fatal consequences" of the document, a group of forty men sign their own resolutions condemning the "said resolves as being repugnant to our ideas of liberty, law, and reason."

❋ **December 16, 1773**—Sam Adams

calls for one last meeting at the Old South Meeting House. A delegation is sent to Governor Hutchinson, asking him to allow the ships to leave without unloading their tea. But Hutchinson, like the other tea agents, has left the city, which gives the colonists their answer. They respond with the Boston Tea Party, dumping all the tea from the three ships into the harbor.

✳ December 17, 1773—Sam Adams sends letters to Cape Cod, urging the local folk to destroy the tea on the stranded ship, the *William*. Jonathan Clarke, the son of Richard Clarke, one of the Boston tea agents, is already on his way to rescue the tea. He has a hard time finding people to help him but finally gets fifty-six chests of the tea into his father's warehouse. Most of this tea is destroyed later, in March 1774.

✳ December 17, 1773—Paul Revere rides to provide news of the Boston Tea Party to the Sons of Liberty in New York and Philadelphia.

✳ December 17, 1773—The Sons of Liberty in New York hold a crowded meeting, their biggest yet, at the town hall to discuss what to do with the tea ship.

✳ December 21, 1773—Paul Revere arrives in New York with the news from Boston.

✳ December 22, 1773—Lieutenant

Governor William Bull has the tea secretly unloaded from the *London* in Charleston Harbor and locked away in the basement of the Old Exchange. It will sit there until war has been declared and then is sold to help pay the costs of fighting against Britain.

✳ December 24, 1773—Paul Revere arrives in Philadelphia with news of the Boston Tea Party.

✳ December 25, 1773—The *Polly* arrives at Chester, near Philadelphia. Members of the Committee for Tarring and Feathering rush to the ship, board it, and threaten Captain Ayres with an "American Exhibition" (meaning tarring and feathering).

✳ December 26, 1773—Committee members escort Captain Ayres to Philadelphia while they discuss what to do with the tea and the ship.

✳ December 27, 1773—In the morning, Captain Ayres visits Thomas Wharton, a tea merchant who has resigned his post as tea agent, fearful of how his neighbors will treat him if he doesn't. Ayres explains to Wharton that if he—and the other tea consignees—won't accept the tea, the captain will register a formal protest. After all, if they won't accept the tea, what choice does he have except to take it all back to London? Wharton understands the need for formalities, and he calls over the other tea agent, Jonathan Browne, along with a

notary. Captain Ayres then repeats his question. Will they accept the tea and pay the tax? The reply is witnessed by the notary: "While the tea belonging to the Honorable East India Company (under your Care) is subject to the Payment of a Duty [tax] in America we cannot Act in the Commission which they have been pleas'd to Honor Us with." Meaning simply, "No."

✳ December 27, 1773—That afternoon, William Bradford and other Sons of Liberty take Ayres to the State House (where the Declaration of Independence will later be signed), where more resolves are made. Ayres will not unload any of his cargo; instead, he will have one day, no more, to stock his ship with the supplies necessary for a return journey to London, and then he has to leave.

✳ December 28, 1773—The *Polly* leaves, with all her original tea still aboard.

✳ March 7, 1774—The last of the tea from the *William* is tracked down and dumped into Boston Harbor at the second Boston Tea Party.

✳ April 18, 1774—The *Nancy*, delayed by bad weather, finally arrives in Sandy Hook, New Jersey, on its way to New York Harbor.

✳ April 22, 1774—The *London*, redirected from Charleston, also arrives in

New York Harbor. The captain denies there is any tea on board. The Sons of Liberty, knowing otherwise, search and find it. They dump all the chests into the harbor.

✳ **April 23, 1774**—A huge angry crowd of New Yorkers confront the captain of the *Nancy* at the Coffee House on Wall Street. The captain leaves on the *Nancy*, with no tea unloaded and the captain from the *London* hidden aboard.

✳ **December 12, 1774**—The *Greyhound*, a much later tea ship, sails up the Delaware River and lands at Greenwich, New Jersey.

✳ **December 22, 1774**—A group of patriots dressed as Indians "liberates" the tea from the *Greyhound* and burns it all in a big bonfire.

Notes

✳ **page 5:** "Men will always go to the cheapest markets." Lord North, in Joseph Cummins, *Ten Tea Parties: Patriotic Protests That History Forgot* (Philadelphia: Quirk Books, 2012), p. 31.

✳ **page 8:** "that threepence on a pound of tea, of which one does not drink perhaps ten pounds a year, is sufficient to overcome the patriotism of an American. . . . They have no idea that people can act from any principle but that of interest." Benjamin Franklin, June 4, 1773, in *Memoirs of Benjamin Franklin*, by Franklin, William Temple Franklin, and William Duane (Philadelphia: McCarty & Davis, 1840), p. 284.

✳ **page 9:** "The hour of destruction, or manly opposition, to the machinations of tyranny, stares you in the face." Boston broadside, 1773, Library of Congress.

✳ **page 12:** "All that we fear, is that you will shrink at Boston. . . . We fear that you will suffer this tea to be landed." *Boston Gazette*, December 13, 1773.

✳ **page 12:** "If you touch one grain of this accursed tea, you are undone. America is threatened with worse than Egyptian slavery." "Alarm," New York handbill, in Francis Samuel Drake, *Tea Leaves: Being a Collection of Letters and Documents Relating to the Shipment of Tea to the American Colonies in the Year 1773*, by the East India Company, (Boston: A. O. Crane, 1884), p. xviii.

✳ **page 19:** "wrest the Towns Ammunition out of the Hands of Col. Knowles." Theresa M. Barbo, "A Bitter Wellfleet Tea Party," in *True Accounts of Yankee Ingenuity and Grit from the "Cape Cod Voice"* (Charleston, S.C.: History Press, 2007), p. 25.

✳ **page 20:** "Every ounce of tea on board was immersed in the Bay, without the least injury to private property. . . ." Cummins, *Ten Tea Parties*, p. 54.

✳ **page 23:** "Captain Ayres . . . ought to have known our people better than to have expected we would be so mean as to suffer his rotten tea to be funneled down our throats with the Parliament's duty mixed with it." Cummins, *Ten Tea Parties*, p. 72.

✳ **page 23:** "To the Delaware Pilots." Philadelphia broadside, Library of Congress, Rare Book and Special Collections Division.

✳ **page 23:** "The Tea-Ship being arrived . . ." Philadelphia broadside, Library of Congress, Rare Book and Special Collections Division.

✳ **page 24:** "that the tea . . . shall not be landed." Resolutions, Philadelphia State House meeting, Monday, December 27, 1773, quoted in John St. George Joyce, ed., *Story of Philadelphia* (Philadelphia: Rex Printing House, 1919), p. 140.

✳ **page 26:** "raise a revenue, out of your pockets, against your consent, and to render assemblies of your representatives totally useless." E. Stanly Godbold Jr. and Robert H. Woody, *Christopher Gadsden and the American Revolution* (Knoxville: University of Tennessee Press, 1982), p. 110.

✳ **page 26:** "light of heaven." Godbold and Woody, *Christopher Gadsden*, p. 110.

❋ **page** 27: "who thought it would be criminal tamely to give up any of our essential rights as British subjects, and involve our posterity in a state little better than slavery." Cummins, *Ten Tea Parties*, pp. 85–86.

❋ **page** 28: "How great then was our chagrin to hear that through some internal division the grand cause was neglected. . . . Must then the liberties of the present and future ages be sacrificed to some unhappy feuds in Carolina?" Merrill Jensen, *The Founding of a Nation: A History of the American Revolution, 1763–1776* (Indianapolis: Hackett, 2004), p. 444.

❋ **page** 28: "that by uniting we stand and by dividing we fall." Jensen, *Founding of a Nation*, p. 444.

❋ **page** 29: "We will not deal with, or employ, or have any connection with him." Jensen, *Founding of a Nation*, p. 445.

❋ **page** 29: "our liberties are equally affected." Jensen, *Founding of a Nation*, p. 445.

❋ **page** 32: "No disguise of any kind was adopted or worn to shelter the person of those who participated in the work from observation or identification. . . ." Abram Wakeman, *1914, New York's Commercial Tercentenary: A Few Historical Events as Given by Historians Compared with Their Actual Occurrence* (New York: Lower Wall Street Business Men's Association, 1914), p.14.

❋ **page** 33: "our mother *in law*." Godbold and Woody, *Christopher Gadsden*, p. 113.

❋ **page** 37: "the muscles of his face previously composed. . . ." *The Critic*, vol. 48, 1906, p. 63.

❋ **page** 38: "tyranny greater than the Roman!" *Franklin Before the Privy Council, White Hall Chapel, London, 1774: On Behalf of the Province of Massachusetts to Advocate the Removal of Hutchinson and Oliver* (Philadelphia: J. M. Butler, 1860). p. 106.

❋ **page** 38: "the whole time like a rock. . . ." James Parton, *Life and Times of Benjamin Franklin*, vol. 1 (New York: Da Capo Press, 1971), p. 592.

❋ **page** 38: "I will make your master. . . ." Andrew M. Allison, Willard Cleon Skousen, and M. Richard Maxfield, *The Real Benjamin Franklin* (Salt Lake City: Freemen Institute, 1982), p. 173.

❋ **page** 38: "reflect on how you are to govern a people. . . ." Edmund Burke, speech on American taxation, 1774, from *The Works of the Right Honourable Edmund Burke*, vol. 1 (London: George Bell and Sons, 1886), p. 434.

❋ **page** 38: "this country [England] has no right under heaven." Basil Williams, *The Life of William Pitt, Earl of Chatham*, vol. 1 (New York: Octagon Books, 1966), p. 299.

❋ **page** 39: "gathered all the steward's winter. . ." *Princeton Alumni Weekly*, vol. 76, 1973, p. 10.

❋ **page** 43: "While the tea belonging to the Honorable East India Company (under your Care). . . ." *The Pennsylvania Magazine of History and Biography*, vol. 14, 1890, p. 78.

Bibliography

Alden, John R. *A History of the American Revolution*. New York: Da Capo Press, 1989.

Allison, Andrew M., William Cleon Skousen, and M. Richard Maxfield. *The Real Benjamin Franklin*. Salt Lake City: Freemen Institute, 1982.

Barbo, Theresa M. "A Bitter Wellfleet Tea Party." In *True Accounts of Yankee Ingenuity and Grit from the "Cape Cod Voice."* Charleston, S.C.: History Press, 2007.

Brandt, Francis Burke. *The Majestic Delaware: The Nation's Foremost Historic River*. Philadelphia: Brandt & Gummere, 1929.

Breen, T. H. *The Marketplace of Revolution*. New York: Oxford University Press, 2004.

Burke, Edmund. *The Works of the Right Honourable Edmund Burke*. London: George Bell and Sons, 1886.

Chestertown Tea Party Festival, annual reenactment. http://www. chestertownteaparty.com.

The Critic, vol. 48, 1906.

Cummins, Joseph. *Ten Tea Parties: Patriotic Protests That History Forgot*. Philadelphia: Quirk Books, 2012.

Drake, Francis Samuel. *Tea Leaves: Being a Collection of Letters and Documents Relating to the Shipment of Tea to the American Colonies in the Year 1773, by the East India Tea Company*. Boston: A. O. Crane, 1884.

Etting, Frank M. *The Philadelphia Tea Party of 1773: A Chapter from the History of the Old State House*. Philadelphia: E. Stern, 1873.

Fleming, Thomas. *Liberty! The American Revolution*. New York: Viking Penguin, 1997.

Franklin Before the Privy Council, White Hall Chapel, London, 1774: On Behalf of the Province of Massachusetts to Advocate the Removal of Hutchinson and Oliver. Philadelphia: John M. Butler, 1859.

Franklin, Benjamin, William Temple Franklin, and William Duane. *Memoirs of Benjamin Franklin*. Philadelphia: McCarty & Davis, 1840.

Gifford, Edward S. Jr. *The American Revolution in the Delaware Valley*. Philadelphia: Pennsylvania Society of Sons of the Revolution, 1976.

Godbold, E. Stanly, Jr., and Robert H. Woody. *Christopher Gadsden and the American Revolution*. Knoxville: University of Tennessee Press, 1982.

Jensen, Merrill. *The Founding of a Nation: A History of the American Revolution, 1763–1776*. Indianapolis: Hackett, 2004.

Joyce, John St. George, ed. *Story of Philadelphia*. Philadelphia: Rex Printing House, 1919.

Kashatus, William C. *Historic Philadelphia: The City, Symbols & Patriots, 1681–1800*. Jefferson, N.C.: McFarland, 1992.

Labaree, Benjamin W. "Boston Tea Party: American Revolution." in United States at War: Understanding Conflict and Society. Santa Barbara, Calif.: ABC-CLIO, January 7, 2009.

Leake, Isaac Q. *Memoir of the Life and Times of General John Lamb*. Albany, N.Y.: Joel Munsell, 1850.

Lossing, Benson J. *Our Country: A Household History for All Readers, from the Discovery of America to the One Hundredth Anniversary of the Declaration of Independence*. New York: Johnson & Miles, 1877.

Miller, Ruth M., and Ann Taylor Andrus. *Charleston's Old Exchange Building: A Witness to American History*. Charleston, S.C.: History Press, 2005.

New York in the Revolution as Colony and State: A Compilation of Documents and Records from the Office of the State Comptroller. Albany, N.Y.: J. B. Lyon, 1904.

Norris, Edwin Mark. *The Story of Princeton*. Boston: Little, Brown, 1917.

Osborne, Anne Riggs. *The South Carolina Story*. Orangeburg, S.C.: Sandlapper, 1932.

Parton, James. *Life and Times of Benjamin Franklin*, vol. 1. New York: Da Capo Press, 1971.

Pennsylvania Magazine of History and Biography, vol. 14, 1890.

Porcher, Frederick A. *A Memoir of Gen. Christopher Gadsden*. Charleston, S.C.: Journal of Commerce Job Office, 1878.

Princeton Alumni Weekly, vol. 76, 1973.

Rosen, Robert. *A Short History of Charleston*. San Francisco: Lexikos, 1982.

Rudy, Willis. *The Campus and a Nation in Crisis: From the American Revolution to Vietnam*. Madison, N.J.: Fairleigh Dickinson University Press, 1996.

Russell, David Lee. *The American Revolution in the Southern Colonies*. Jefferson, N.C.: McFarland, 2000.

Ulmann, Albert. "The Tea Party New York Had." *New York Times*, January 21, 1899.

Wakeman, Abram. *1914, New York's Commercial Tercentenary: A Few Historical Events as Given by Historians Compared with Their Actual Occurrence*. New York: Lower Wall Street Business Men's Association, 1914.

Wellcome, Henry Solomon. *The Story of Metlakahtla*. London and New York: Saxon, 1887.

Williams, Basil. *The Life of William Pitt, Earl of Chatham*, vol. 1. New York: Octagon Books, 1966.

Wilson, Robert H. *Philadelphia: Official Handbook for Visitors*. Maplewood, N.J.: C. S. Hammond, 1964.

Illustration Credits

Index

Note: Page numbers in *italics* refer to illustrations.